Do you know what the words below mean? Record yo[ur]
thoughts about each meaning, then look up the words
in a dictionary.

I think this word means ...

The definition in the dictionary is ...

orphan

rebellious

provocation

composure

agitated

Read Chapter 1 of *Oliver Twist*. Record your thoughts about each of the three questions in the spaces below.

The looking question is …
Why were the boys' food rations so light?

The clue question is …
Why did the boys draw lots to see who would ask for more gruel?

The thinking question is …
Why do you think Oliver kept his dreams of a family to himself?

Do you have any questions? Write them here.

Think about the conversations you have had about this text. What more have you learned? Complete the activity below.

Do you think the workhouse was a suitable place for children? Give reasons for your answer.

What do we know about Oliver Twist? Write three words to describe Oliver and explain why you chose those words in the spaces provided.

I think Oliver is ...

I think this because ...

I think Oliver is ...

I think this because ...

I think Oliver is ...

I think this because ...

Feedback

Put each word into the correct sentence.

acutely   handkerchief   slumped   reverie

circumstances   trudge   gawping

overwhelmed   astonishment

Lost in a .... , I did not hear my friend calling my name.

When she missed the last bus, the lady had to .... across town carrying her heavy shopping bags.

Sat in the corner of the library, the elderly gentleman used a silk .... to blow his nose.

The young actress was .... when she won the best new actress award.

Charlie did an excellent job of his homework in the difficult
....

To his .... Jack was chosen to play on the school football team.

As the dazzling, colourful carnival floats drove by, the little girl sat .... at the amazing sight.

As the gymnast took his position on the beam he was
.... aware of the judges' eyes watching him.

After a long exhausting day, the doctor .... into a cosy armchair and kicked off her shoes.

Use the bold words to write your own sentences in the spaces provided.

He sat down, dazed and **exhausted**.

The gentleman was horrified at the thought of the **injustice**.

"Actually it's business I'm 'ere about," said Nancy, **briskly**.

The stranger listened **intently**, nodding thoughtfully from time to time.

Read Chapter 2 of *Oliver Twist*. Record your thoughts about each of the three questions in the spaces below.

The looking question is ...
How is Oliver feeling when he arrives in London?

The clue question is ...
Is Dodger being kind when he offers Oliver a place to stay?

The thinking question is ...
Where do you think Oliver was better off: in the workhouse, or when he was staying with Fagin?

Do you have any questions? Write them here.

Think about the conversations you have had about this text. What more have you learned? Complete the activities below.

Imagine and describe how Oliver is feeling when he arrives in London.

Speculate on why Dodger offers Oliver a place to stay and introduces him to Fagin.

Discuss whether Oliver has ever had a proper home.

Think about the text you have read. Write your own looking, clue and thinking questions in the spaces below.

Feedback

Can you remember these words from Chapter 2? Write
two sentences using each word in the spaces below.

astonishment

overwhelmed

acutely

gawping

Which words or phrases have a similar meaning to the focus word? Write them in the spaces below.

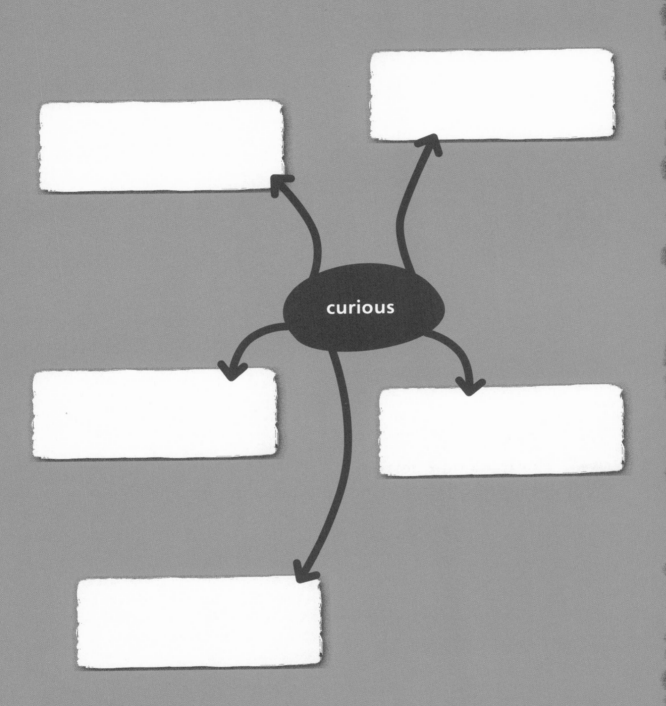

Read Chapter 3 of *Oliver Twist*. Record your thoughts about each of the three questions in the spaces below.

The looking question is ...
Why is Oliver kidnapped?

The clue question is ...
Who do you think the lady in the portrait could be?

The thinking question is ...
Who are Oliver's friends and who are his enemies?

Do you have any questions? Write them here.

Think about the conversations you have had about this text. What more have you learned? Complete the activity below.

Imagine you are Oliver. Which character do you feel safest with? Give reasons for your answer.

What do you think will happen next? Write your prediction in the space below.

I predict ...

Feedback

Change each word so that it fits in the sentences. Write your answers in the spaces provided.

protector

Cyclists wear a helmet to .... their head from injuries.

Police officers wear bulletproof vests as .... from gunshots.

Sat behind the windbreak on the beach, we were .... from the weather.

secretive

.... Jack hoped that the toy car was for him and not his brother.

Could the children keep the surprise party a ....?

They .... decorated the village hall with balloons ready for the party.

suspicions

Her brother had been behaving .... all day.

Henry began to .... that his sister was up to something.

It was a little .... that everyone arrived at the same time.

Read the text and complete the activities below.

The police had launched an investigation into a vicious crime. The news reporters loitered outside while the police gathered enough evidence to confirm their suspicions. What could have provoked the attack? The atmosphere outside the police station grew tense.

Find and copy the word that means "waited".

What does the word "vicious" tell you about the crime?

Think of a synonym for the word "provoked".

Read Chapter 4 of *Oliver Twist*. Record your thoughts about each of the three questions in the spaces below.

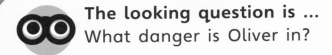 **The looking question is ...**
What danger is Oliver in?

The clue question is ...
Why does Nancy talk to Mr Brownlow and Rose Maylie?

The thinking question is ...
Is Dodger's punishment fair?

Do you have any questions? Write them here.

Think about the conversations you have had about this text. What more have you learned? Complete the activities below

Explain Fagin's plans for Oliver.

Argue that Nancy is foolish to try to help Oliver.

Discuss whether Dodger deserves to be shipped to Australia.

Summarise what happens in Chapter 4 of *Oliver Twist*, using the flowchart below.

Mrs Maylie and her niece ...

Back in London ...

Nancy overheard ...

She met with Mr Brownlow and Rose and ...

Back at Fagin's ...

Charley followed Bill and ...

Feedback

Do you know what the words below mean? Record your thoughts about each meaning, then look up the words in a dictionary.

I think this word means ...

The definition in the dictionary is ...

reluctance

remarkable

coincidence

accusation

revelation

Which words or phrases have a similar meaning to the focus word? Write them in the spaces below.

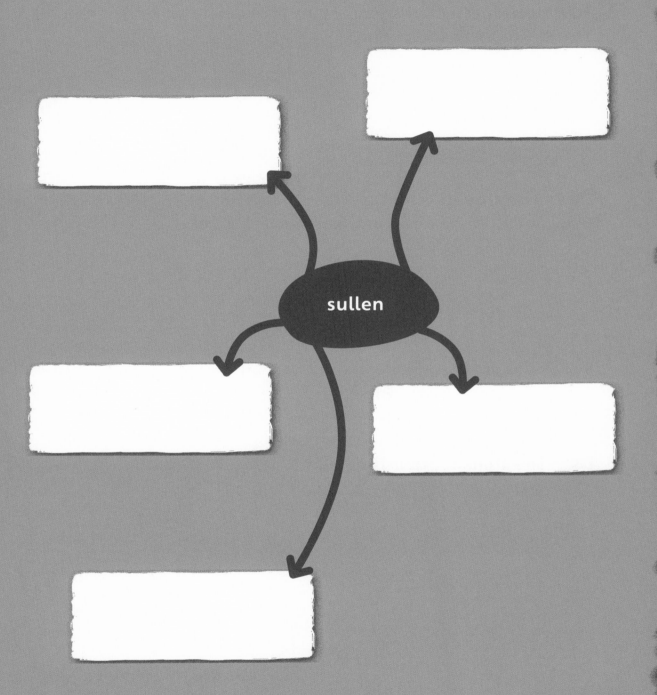

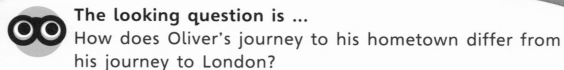
Read Chapter 5 of *Oliver Twist*. Record your thoughts about each of the three questions in the spaces below.

The looking question is ...
How does Oliver's journey to his hometown differ from his journey to London?

The clue question is ...
Why did Monks want to remove all traces of Oliver's identity?

The thinking question is ...
Does the story have a happy ending? Why?

Do you have any questions? Write them here.

Think about the conversations you have had about this text. What more have you learned? Complete the activity below.

Compare and contrast Oliver's circumstances at the beginning and end of the story.

Imagine you are talking to the author of *Oliver Twist*. Write down what you liked about the text and two things you would change.

I liked ...

I would change ...

I would change ...

Feedback

Put each word into the correct sentence.

runaways   ducked   fretting   debt

lantern   patrolled   mercy   quilt

I was so busy .... about my exam, I walked right past the school.

I owed my brother £4 and I was not allowed to borrow his bike until I'd paid my ....

The two .... decided to come back home when it got dark.

The thief begged the shopkeeper for .... saying her children were hungry.

The cabin was old and dirty but by the light of the .... it looked cosy.

My grandmother used scraps from my old dresses to make a .... for my bed.

We hid behind the mound and watched as the soldiers .... the outside of the base with their dogs.

Poppy and Sam .... as the ball came whizzing towards them.

Do you know what the words below mean? Record your thoughts about each meaning, then look up the words in a dictionary.

I think this word means ...

The definition in the dictionary is ...

auction

pallet

deliverance

gourd

plantation

Read Chapters 1 and 2 of *The Road to Freedom*.
Record your thoughts about each of the three questions
in the spaces below.

The looking question is ...
What triggers Mama's decision to run away?

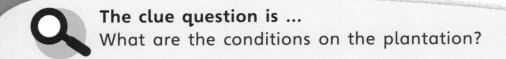

The clue question is ...
What are the conditions on the plantation?

The thinking question is ...
Were Mama and Emma wrong to run away?

Do you have any questions? Write them here.

Think about the conversations you have had about this text. What more have you learned? Complete the activities below.

Argue that freedom is more important than safety.

Discuss how the master could run his plantation without slaves.

Speculate on how one person can feel it is right to own another.

How do you think each character will feel about the dangers of being a runaway? Write your predictions in the spaces provided.

Feedback

Explore the verb "to track" by completing the activities below.

Look up the focus word in the dictionary.

Make up a sentence using the focus word.

track
(verb)

Write two synonyms for the focus word.

What is the connection between the verb "track" and the noun "track"?

Can you remember these words from Chapters 1 and 2?
Write two sentences using each word in the spaces below.

auction

plantation

mercy

fretting

Read Chapters 3 and 4 of *The Road to Freedom*. Record your thoughts about each of the three questions in the spaces below.

The looking question is ...
What problems do Mama and Emma face on their journey?

The clue question is ...
Why isn't the old woman surprised to see Mama and Emma?

The thinking question is ...
How do slaves find out about the old woman's house?

Do you have any questions? Write them here.

Think about the conversations you have had about this text. What more have you learned? Complete the activities below.

Imagine you are Emma hiding in the leaves from the dogs. How do you feel?

Explain whether or not you think a lantern and a quilt are good signs to use.

Argue that the route is too dangerous and too unknown to be worth attempting.

What were the consequences of each event in the text?
Write your answers in the spaces below.

There is a storm and it pours with rain.

Consequence ...

The old woman hangs a quilt over the fence.

Consequence ...

Feedback

What can you find out about the Underground Railroad? Complete the activities below.

What was the Underground Railroad?

When did the Underground Railroad begin and end?

Underground Railroad

Name one person who is famous for their work on the Underground Railroad.

Why do you think it was called the Underground Railroad?

Look at the pictures and the words, then look up the words in the dictionary. What do they mean? Write a definition in your own words in the spaces below.

Quaker

My Notes

My Notes

enslave

slats

My Notes

My Notes

reins

Read Chapter 5 of *The Road to Freedom*. Record your thoughts about each of the three questions in the spaces below.

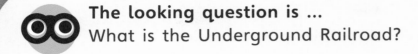
The looking question is ...
What is the Underground Railroad?

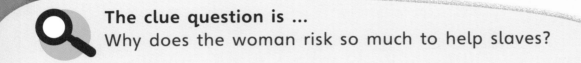
The clue question is ...
Why does the woman risk so much to help slaves?

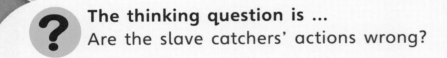
The thinking question is ...
Are the slave catchers' actions wrong?

Do you have any questions? Write them here.

Think about the conversations you have had about this text. What more have you learned? Complete the activities below.

Speculate on the different people and resources needed to run the Underground Railroad.

How do you think each character will feel about Mama and Emma's escape from the slave catchers? Write your predictions in the spaces below.

Feedback

Use the bold words and phrases to write your own sentences in the spaces provided.

The **mules** whinnied next to the wagon.

"Yessir . . . I mean no, sir," the driver **stuttered**.

We pulled two **bales** of hay in front of us and lay down to wait.

It felt like the wagon hit every stone and **rut** as we travelled along.

Can you remember these words from earlier in the story? Write two sentences using each word in the spaces below.

track (verb)

enslave

debt

deliverance

Read Chapters 6 and 7 of *The Road to Freedom*.
Record your thoughts about each of the three questions
in the spaces below.

The looking question is ...
In what ways does the wagon driver help Mama
and Emma?

The clue question is ...
How did Emma feel travelling in the potato wagon?

The thinking question is ...
Why do some people need to escape to freedom
in the world today, and how do they do this?

Do you have any questions? Write them here.

Think about the conversations you have had about this text. What more have you learned? Complete the activity below.

Discuss whether or not people should be allowed to travel freely around the world.

What do you think will happen next? Write your prediction in the space below.

I predict ...

Feedback

Do you know what the words and phrases below mean?
Record your thoughts about each meaning, then look up the
words and phrases in a dictionary.

I think this
word means ...

The definition in
the dictionary is ...

bounty hunters

depot

territory

dawned

Explore the focus word by completing the activities below.

Look up the focus word in a dictionary and write a definition.

Make up a sentence using the focus word.

hunched

Write some synonyms for the focus word. Circle the best match.

Write an antonym for the focus word.

Read Chapter 8 and 9 of *The Road to Freedom*.
Record your thoughts about each of the three questions in the spaces below.

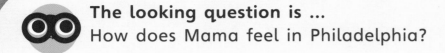
The looking question is ...
How does Mama feel in Philadelphia?

The clue question is ...
Why was there a huge reward for the capture of Harriet Tubman?

The thinking question is ...
Why did Harriet choose to help so many people?

Do you have any questions? Write them here.

Think about the conversations you have had about this text. What more have you learned? Complete the activities below.

Describe how you change when you are happy.

Argue that Harriet's reward was justified.

Why were Harriet's actions considered to be so brave?

Imagine you are interviewing Harriet Tubman about how she rescued so many slaves. What questions would you ask? Write three questions on the clipboard below.

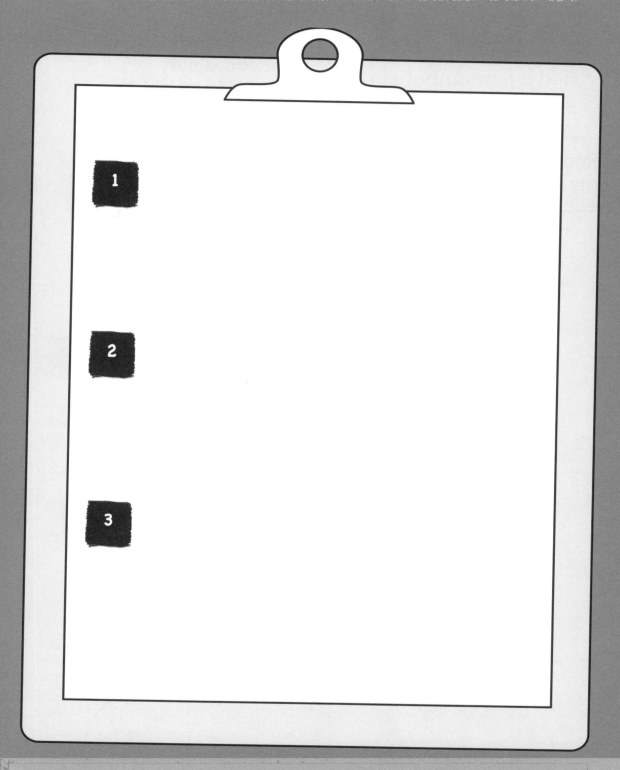

1

2

3

Feedback

Reading Goals

This term I aim to …

Find a new author I like!

Read a play with friends!

Read the book of my favourite film!

Learn a poem by heart!

Group Discussion Rules

- We will listen carefully to the person who is speaking

- Everyone should have a chance to speak

- We will give reasons for our ideas

- We can ask others for reasons if they don't say them

- **We can agree and disagree politely with each other**

- We will respect each other's ideas and opinions

- We will share all the information in the group

- We will try to reach an agreement together if we can

Add any other group discussion rules your class or group has decided on here:

- ....

- ....

- ....

- ....

- ....

Reading Tracker

Book title: ....

Author: ....

Date finished: .... Score out of 10 ☐

Book title: ....

Author: ....

Date finished: .... Score out of 10 ☐

Book title: ....

Author: ....

Date finished: .... Score out of 10 ☐

Book title: ....

Author: ....

Date finished: .... Score out of 10 ☐

Book title: ....

Author: ....

Date finished: .... Score out of 10 ☐

Book title: ....

Author: ....

Date finished: .... Score out of 10 ☐

Book title: ....

Author: ....

Date finished: .... Score out of 10 ☐

Book title: ....

Author: ....

Date finished: .... Score out of 10 ☐

Book title: ....

Author: ....

Date finished: .... Score out of 10 ☐

Book title: ....

Author: ....

Date finished: .... Score out of 10 ☐

Read-alikes

If you liked liked *Oliver Twist*, why not try ...

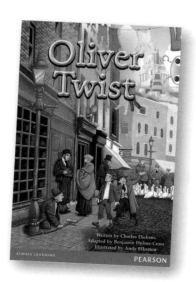

Henry's Freedom Box
by Ellen Levine

Chains
by Lauren Halse Anderson

If you liked *The Road to Freedom*, why not try ...

I Was a Rat!
by Philip Pullman

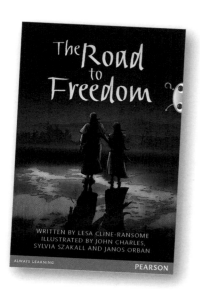

Rooftoppers
by Katherine Rundell

Tick the types of text you have read this term!

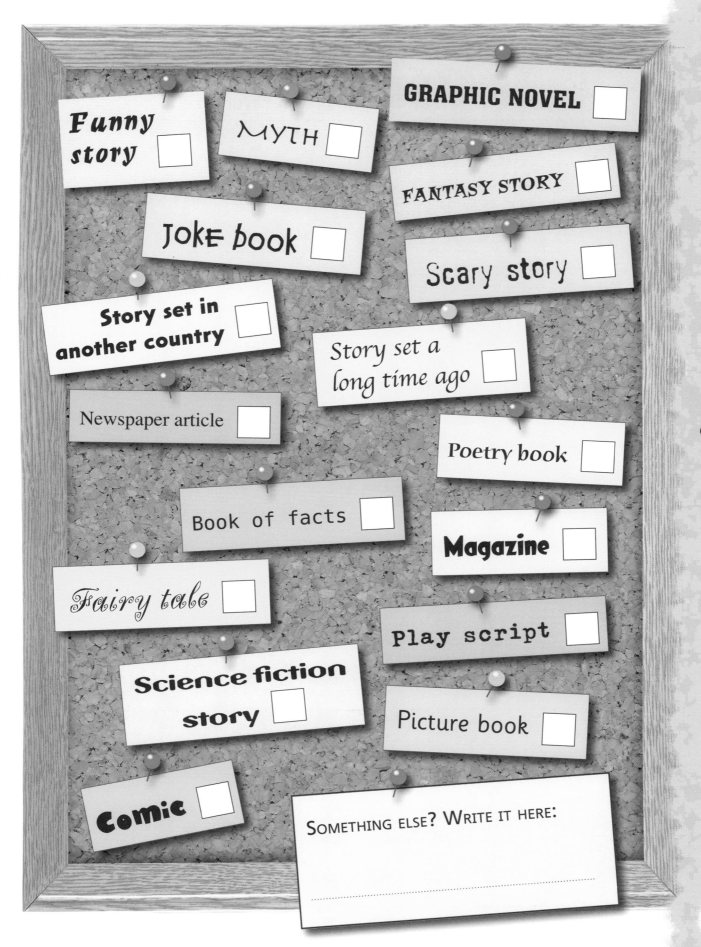

GRAPHIC NOVEL ☐

Funny story ☐

MYTH ☐

FANTASY STORY ☐

JOKE book ☐

Scary story ☐

Story set in another country ☐

Story set a long time ago ☐

Newspaper article ☐

Poetry book ☐

Book of facts ☐

Magazine ☐

Fairy tale ☐

Play script ☐

Science fiction story ☐

Picture book ☐

Comic ☐

SOMETHING ELSE? WRITE IT HERE:

....

The best new words I have learned this term

Word	What it means
revelation	a surprising and previously unknown fact that has been revealed

The best jokes I have read this term

Did you hear about the hungry clock?

It went back four seconds.

Reading Record

Fill in these sheets for one story you have chosen yourself.

At the beginning

Title:

Author:

Why did you choose this book?

What score do you think you'll give it? | /10 |

Who is the character you like most?

Has anything like this ever happened to you?

What questions do you have about the story?

What do you think will happen at the end?

At the end

Were your predictions right?

Is there anything that still puzzles you?

What score would you give this book? | /10 |

Who do you think would enjoy this book?

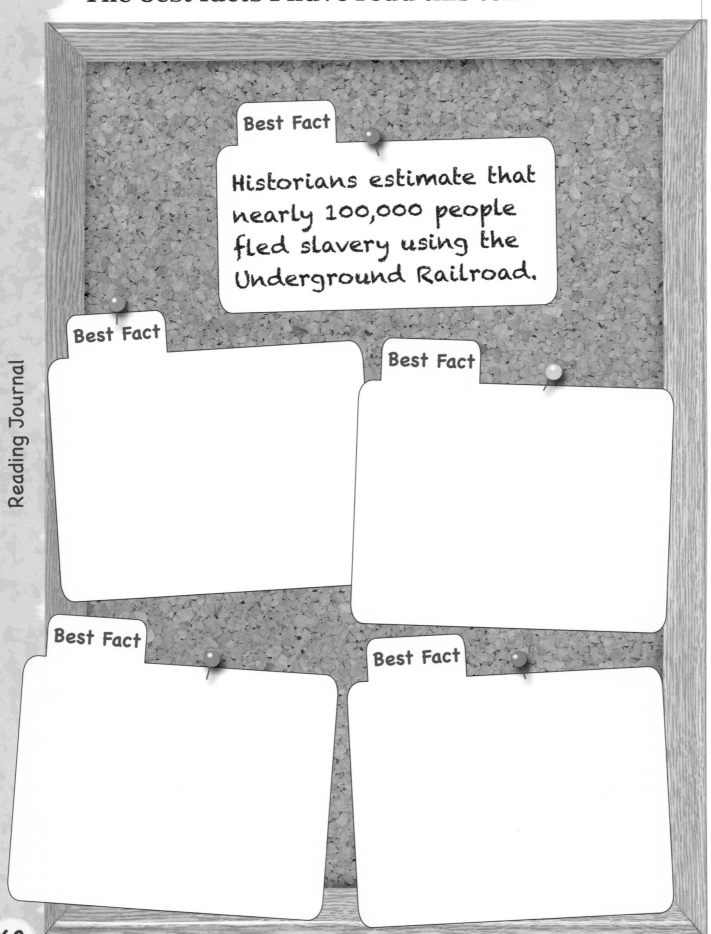

Best Fact

Historians estimate that nearly 100,000 people fled slavery using the Underground Railroad.

Best Fact

Best Fact

Best Fact

Best Fact

Reading Journal